This resource is for speakers of English who want to learn **Austrian** German without first having to learn Standard German.

As far as I am aware, there are no resources available for these learners, at least in English. Other resources describe Austrian only in terms of how it differs from Standard German – and so a knowledge of Standard German is assumed and required. In contrast, this book makes **no reference to Standard German at all**. It starts with Austrian as a complete language in itself.

Describing a language is complex, even when that language is standardized. Describing a dialect of that language is even more complex, because dialects – by definition – are not standardized. This book therefore presents only a **standardized** form of Austrian, based on the language spoken in Vienna. It does not aim to describe all the many and varied features of all the dialects and accents of Austria. Rather, it presents a single arbitrary standard, which would be required if Austrian had the status of a language.

All the example words in the next section and all the answer sections in this book have FREE accompanying audio files.

To listen to the audio files, please visit
tinyurl.com/2s4ep29z

Contents

A note on pronunciation   1

Part One: Categories   **7**

Nouns   9
Determiners   21
Prepositions   29
Pronouns   37
Adjectives   45
Adverbs   53
Verbs   63
Conjunctions   69
Numbers   75

Part Two: More about verbs   **83**

Verbs with du, *es* and i   85
Special verbs   91
Creating nouns   97
Creating adjectives   103
Inverting   111

Negating	117
Separating	121
Ghosting	127
Instructing	133

Part Three: More about nouns and adjectives   **137**

Formalizing	139
Sheep and wolves	145
Possessing	157
Comparing	161
Donating	167
Ghosting nouns	171
Parachuting	175
Combining	179
Misgendering	185
Identifying	189
Vanishing	195
Respecting	199

A note on pronunciation

Unlike in English, there is pretty consistent relationship between letters and sounds in Austrian. The following letters represent the following approximate sounds (using symbols from the International Phonetic Alphabet):

SPELLING	SOUND	EXAMPLE
a	a	Kastl
ach	ax	Shuach
ai	aj	Baisl
au	aw	Baua
b	b	Biachl
c	tʃ	Cik
ch	ç	Debich
d	d	Soidot
dj	dʒ	Djob
e	e	Bet
f	f	Fish
g	g	Goatn
h	h	Huat
i	i	Fich
j	j	Joguat
jh	ʒ	Orojhn
k	k	Karotn
l	l	Limone
m	m	Madl
n	n	Nudl
ng	ŋ	Retung
o	o	Gros

1

och	ox	No**ch**bo
oi	oj	S**oi**z
ö	ø	L**ö**ve
p	p	**Sh**piagl
pf	pf	O**pf**l
r	r	**R**ais
s	s	**S**enga
sh	ʃ	**Sh**oklad
u	u	K**u**chn
ü	Y	Fam**ü**lie
v	v	**V**ind
x	ks	Ha**x**n
z	ts	Ko**z**

When two consonants appear next to each other that might be difficult to pronounce, you may hear an extremely short ə between them:

Gmias
vegetables
(gəmias)

Madl
girl
(madəl)

Did you know?

Probably the only Austrian <u>consonant</u> sounds most English speakers might have trouble with are x and ç. The sound x in fact occurs in many varieties of English, such as at the end of Scottish lo**ch** and in the Liverpool accent:

    noch   duach
    no**x**   dua**x**

The sound ç also often occurs in English at the beginning of the word **h**uge:

    Richta   shprechn
    riçta   ʃpreçən

Did you know?

Probably the only Austrian <u>vowel</u> sounds most English speakers might have trouble with are ø and ʏ. The sound ø is essentially e but with the lips rounded. It sounds pretty close to the English interjection urgh:

    Östaraich   vöche
    østarajç   vøçə
    (ə:starajç)   (və:çə)

The sound ʏ is essentially i but with the lips rounded. It sounds pretty close to the English interjection ew:

    Brün   Müch
    brʏn   mʏç
    (bru:n)   (mu:ç)

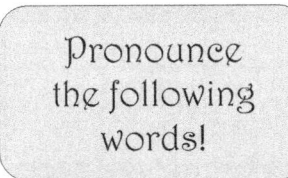

Pronounce the following words!

Löve

Shlisl

Gmias

Zvecke

Zvucgl

Soidot

Pflonzn

Gnofe

Shlongn

Haisl

🔊

> Here are the answers. No cheating!

Löve
löve

Soidot
sojdot

Shlisl
ʃlisəl

Pflonzn
pflontsən

Gmias
gəmijas

Gnofe
gnofe

Zvecke
tsvetʃke

Shlongn
ʃloŋən

Zvucgl
tsvutʃgəl

Haisl
hajsəl

Part One: Categories

Nouns

Nouns refer to things:

Doshn	bag
Fro	woman
Kanikl	rabbit
Koz	cat
Opfl	apple
Shtot	city

To pluralize, make the noun end in n:

SINGULAR	PLURAL
Fro woman	Fron women
Koz cat	Kozn cats
Karotn carrot	Karotn carrots

Many plural forms are unpredictable:

SINGULAR	PLURAL
Opfl apple	**Epfl** apples
Mon man	**Mena** men

The following are some common nouns:

ambulance	Retung
architect (male)	Achitekt
astronaut (male)	Astronot
aunt	Dont
baby	Zvucgl
bag	Sakl
banana	Banane
bean	Bondl
bear	Bea
bed	Bet
bee	Bine
book	Biachl
bottle	Floshn
box	Kistn
bucket	Kiabl
butter	Buta
cake	Kuchn
carrot	Karotn
cat	Koz
chair	Sesl
cherry	Kiashn
chocolate	Shoklad
clothes	Gvond
cloud	Voikn
cucumber	Guakn

desert	Viastn
door	Dia
ear	Oavashl
elephant	Elefont
eye	Og
family	Famülie
farmer (male)	Baua
fire	Faia
flower	Bleaml
food	Lebnsmitl
fork	Gobl
fruit	Obst
garlic	Gnofe
girl	Madl
glasses (spectacles)	Brün
grape	Vanpl
grass	Gros
head	Shedl
house	Haisl
husband	Gate
ice	Ais
island	Insl
key	Shlisl
kitchen	Kuchl
lake	Se
lamp	Lompn
leg	Haxn
lemon	Limone
lion	Löve
meat	Flaish
milk	Müch
mirror	Shpiagl
monkey	Of
mouth	Goshl
nature	Natua
nose	Nosn

onion	Zvife
parents	Ötan
pasta	Nudl
photo	Büdl
pilot (male)	Bilot
plant	Pflonzn
plum	Zvecke
police officer (female)	Bolites
profession	Hakn
raspberry	Himbea
rice	Rais
salt	Soiz
shelf	Kastl
sister	Shvesta
sky	Himl
snail	Shnek
snake	Shlongn
snow	Shne
sock	Sokn
soldier (male)	Soidot
soup	Supn
spoon	Lefl
staircase	Shtiagn
star	Shtean
storm	Shtuam
student (male)	Shtudent
sun	Sun
trousers	Hosen
uncle	Onkl
vegetables	Gmias
wife	Fro
wind	Vind
woman	Fro

The following are some common nouns with unpredictable plural forms. The following nouns add *e* in the plural:

arm	Oam	Oame
boat	Bot	Bote
bus	Bus	Buse
carpet	Debich	Debiche
king	König	Könige
moon	Mond	Monde
salad	Salot	Salote
sheep	Shof	Shofe

The following nouns add *a* in the plural:

animal	Fich	Ficha
bag	Doshn	Doshna
child	Kind	Kinda
egg	Ai	Aia
face	Gsicht	Gsichta
tree	Bam	Bama

The following nouns add *s* in the plural:

avocado	Avokado	Avokados
car	Oto	Otos
tea	De	Des
yogurt	Joguat	Joguats

The following nouns add en in the plural. Note that these all refer to women:

architect	Achitektin	Achitektinen
artist	Künstlerin	Künstlerinen
astronaut	Astronotin	Astronotinen
dancer	Denzerin	Denzerinen
doctor	Eaztin	Eaztinen
friend	Fraindin	Fraindinen
hairdresser	Friserin	Friserinen
judge	Richterin	Richterinen
neighbor	Nochbarin	Nochbarinen
pilot	Bilotin	Bilotinen
plumber	Inshtalaterin	Inshtalaterinen
queen	Königin	Königinen
secretary	Sekreterin	Sekreterinen
singer	Sengerin	Sengerinen
soldier	Soidotin	Soidotinen
student	Shtudentin	Shtudentinen
teacher	Lererin	Lererinen
waitress	Könerin	Könerinen

The following nouns change o to e in the plural:

apple	Opfl	Epfl
beach	Shtrond	Shtrend
beard	Boat	Beat
bird	Fogl	Fegl
city	Shtot	Shtet
coat	Montl	Mentl
father	Foda	Feda
floor	Fuasbodn	Fuasbedn
garden	Goatn	Geatn

grandfather	Grosfoda	Grosfeda
hand	Hond	Hend
juice	Soft	Seft
mouse	Mos	Mes
potato	Eadopfl	Eadepfl
rainbow	Regnbogn	Regnbegn
sofa	Bonk	Benk
wall	Vond	Vend

The following nouns change u to i in the plural:

brother	Bruada	Briada
cow	Kua	Kia
foot	Fuas	Fias
grandmother	Grosmuada	Grosmiada
hat	Huat	Hiat
mother	Muada	Miada

The following nouns are unpredictable in the plural:

ball	Boi	**Boine**
boy	Bua	**Buam**
doctor (male)	Oazt	**Eazte**
forest	Void	**Vöda**
frog	Grot	**Grotna**
hairdresser (male)	Frisea	**Frisere**
horse	Ros	**Röse**
man	Mon	**Mena**
neighbor (male)	Nochbo	**Nochban**
plumber (male)	Inshtalatea	**Inshtalatere**
sea	Mea	**Mere**
secretary	Sekretea	**Sekretere**
shirt	Hemad	**Hemdn**

son	Bua	**Buam**
stone	Shta	**Shtane**
tooth	Zon	**Zent**
train	Zug	**Ziag**
wardrobe	Kostn	**Kestn**
wolf	Voif	**Vöf**

The following nouns don't change in the plural:

airplane	Flugzaig	Flugzaig
artist (male)	Künstler	Künstler
bedroom	Shlofzima	Shlofzima
bicycle	Radl	Radl
biscuit	Keks	Keks
body	Köpa	Köpa
cauliflower	Kafiol	Kafiol
cheese	Kas	Kas
chicken	Hendl	Hendl
cigarette	Cik	Cik
coffee	Kafe	Kafe
computer	Kompjuta	Kompjuta
cup	Hefl	Hefl
cushion	Boista	Boista
dancer (male)	Denza	Denza
daughter	Menca	Menca
deer	Re	Re
dog	Hund	Hund
eggplant	Melanzani	Melanzani
finger	Finga	Finga
fish	Fish	Fish
friend (male)	Havara	Havara
glove	Handshuach	Handshuach
hair	Hoa	Hoa
honey	Honig	Honig

jacket	Jompa	Jompa
judge (male)	Richta	Richta
knife	Mesa	Mesa
lizard	Aidaxl	Aidaxl
mechanic (male)	Mechanika	Mechanika
mountain	Beag	Beag
mushroom	Shvaml	Shvaml
octopus	Dintnfish	Dintnfish
oil	Ö	Ö
orange	Orojhn	Orojhn
peach	Pfeshe	Pfeshe
pineapple	Ananas	Ananas
plate	Döla	Döla
police officer (male)	Kivara	Kivara
rabbit	Kanikl	Kanikl
river	Flus	Flus
room	Zima	Zima
ship	Shif	Shif
shoe	Shuach	Shuach
singer (male)	Senga	Senga
spice	Gviaz	Gviaz
table	Dish	Dish
teacher (male)	Lere	Lere
tomato	Baradaisa	Baradaisa
turnip	Ruam	Ruam
vehicle	Foazaig	Foazaig
waiter (male)	Köna	Köna
window	Fensta	Fensta

Pluralize the following nouns!

Bine
bee

———
bees

Hemad
shirt

———
shirts

Boista
cushion

———
cushions

Kua
cow

——
cows

Soidotin
soldier (female)

————
soldiers (female)

Here are the answers. No cheating!

Bine
bee

Binen
bees

Hemad
shirt

Hemdn
shirts

Boista
cushion

Boista
cushions

Kua
cow

Kia
cows

Soidotin
soldier (female)

Soidotin**en**
soldiers (female)

Determiners

DETERMINERS appear before nouns:

Koz
cat

jede Koz
each cat

Epfl
apples

a boa Epfl
a few apples

Unlike in English, we use different possessive determiners depending on whether there is one possession or multiple possessions:

mai
my (one possession)

mai Shvesta
my sister

maine
my (multiple possessions)

maine Shvestan
my sisters

The following are some common determiners:

a, an	a
no (singular)	ka
no (plural)	kane
a few	a boa
a few	venige
a few, a little	venig
a few, some	anige
a little	a bisl
a little	a veng
a little	a vengl
all, all the (selection)	semtliche
all, all the (total)	ole
all, all the	oi de
both	de baiden
each, every	jede
enough	gnua
fewer, less	veniga
how many?, how much?	vi fü?
how many?, how much?	vi füle?
many	füle
many a	monch
many a	monche
many, much	fü
more	mea
several	etliche

several	merere
some ... or other	iagendvöche
such	so
such, that kind of	daglaichn
such a	so a
the	de
this, these, that, those	de ... do
umpteen	zig
what!	vos fia!
what a!	vos fia a!
what kind of?	vos fia?
what kind of? (singular)	vos fia a?
what?, which?	vöche?

The following determiners are used with one possession:

my	mai
our	unsa
his, its	sai
her	ia
their	ia
your (one owner)	dai
your (multiple owners)	aicha

The following determiners are used with multiple possessions:

my	maine
our	unsare
his, its	saine
her	ire
their	ire
your (one owner)	daine
your (multiple owners)	aichare

Did you know?

The determiners de and a do not always match their English equivalents:

si libt **de** Musik
she loves music
(she loves the music)

i hob ma **de** Hoa gvoshn
I have washed my hair
(I have me washed the hair)

de Maria
Maria
(the Maria – with first names)

noch kuaza Foat
after a short journey
(after short journey)

si is Eaztin
she is a doctor
(she is doctor)

si is **a** guade Eaztin
she is a good doctor
(she is a good doctor)

Match the determiners!

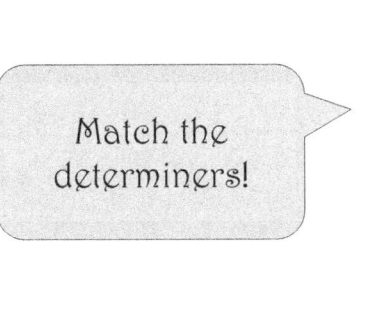

a bisl					your

aicha					my

maine					a little

merere					no

ka					several

Here are the answers. No cheating!

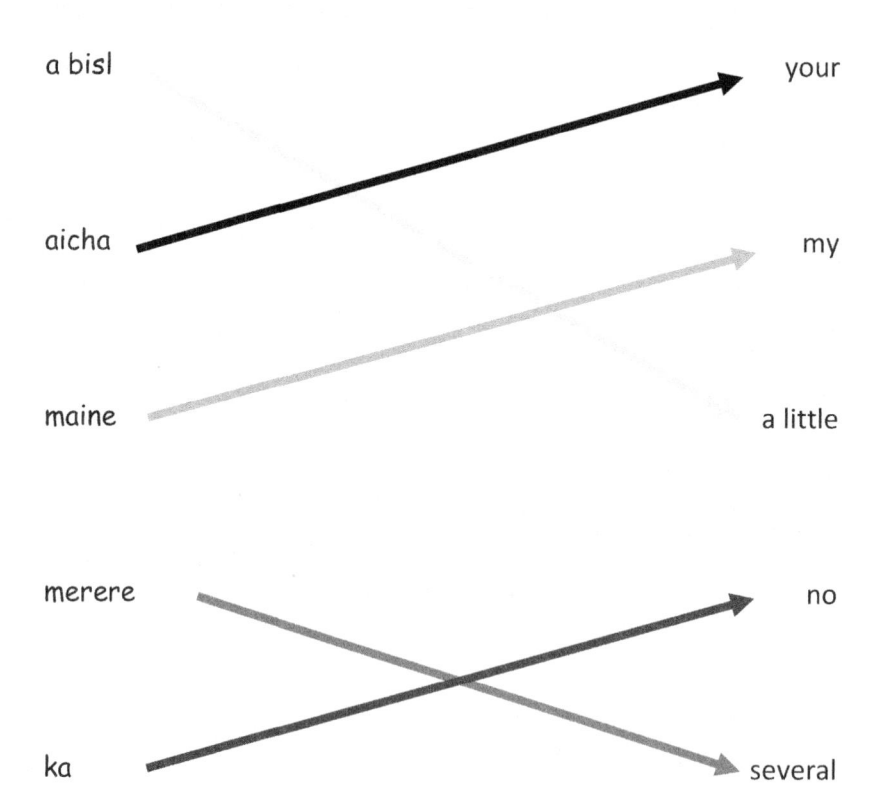

a bisl — your

aicha — my

maine — a little

merere — no

ka — several

Prepositions

Prepositions appear before determiners:

    a Koz   **one** a Koz
    a cat   without a cat

    de Mena   **fia** de Mena
    the men   for the men

Some prepositions are special. After these prepositions, we change any final *e* of a determiner to a:

    fia   fia de Koz
    for   for the cat

    fo   fo da Koz
    from   from the cat

We also change the following determiners:

a	an**a**
ka	kan**a**
mai	main**a**
sai	sain**a**
dai	dain**a**
unsa	uns**ara**
ia	i**ara**
aicha	aich**ara**

mai	one mai Koz
my	without my cat
noch	noch **maina** Koz
toward	toward my cat

The following are some common prepositions:

above (direction)	üva
about (topic)	üva
across, over (direction)	üva
against	gegn
around (approximate time)	gegn
around (place)	um
as a, in the role of a	ois
at (clock time)	um
at (direction)	on
behind (direction)	hinta
below, under (direction)	unta
between (direction)	zvishn
by (by means of)	duach
for	fia
in exchange for	gegn
in front of (direction)	fua
in, inside, into (direction)	in
next to (direction)	nebn
on (direction)	of
through (place)	duach
throughout (time)	duach
until (time and place)	bis
with or without	mit oda one
without	one

The following are some common special prepositions:

above (position)	ovahoib fo
above (position)	üva
according to	noch
across, over (position)	üva
after (time)	noch
among (position)	unta
at (position)	on
at, by (place)	bai
because of	vegn
before (time)	fua
behind (position)	hinta
below (position)	untahoib fo
below, under (position)	unta
between (position)	zvishn
beyond (position)	hinta
by (performed by someone)	fo
by (transport)	mit
during	verend
except, except for	osa
for (duration)	sait
for (purpose)	zua
from	fo
from (origin)	os
in front of (position)	fua
in, inside, into (position)	in
inside of (position)	inahoib fo
instead of	shtot
made of	os
next to (position)	nebn
of (ownership)	fo

on (day)	on
on (position)	of
opposite	gegnüva
out of	os
outside of (position)	osahoib fo
since	sait
to (countries, towns)	noch
to (places, occasions)	zua
towards	noch
with	mit

Fill in the blanks!

sai
his

Des Gshenk do is fia ___ Muada.
This present is for his mother.

vöche?
which?

Os _____ Shtot kumst du?
Which city do you come from?

ia
her

Ole san kema, osa _____ Shvesta.
Everyone came except her sister.

de
the

De Mos is in ___ Kuchl glofn.
The mouse ran into the kitchen.

> Here are the answers. No cheating!

sai
his

Des Gshenk do is fia sai Muada.
This present is for his mother.

vöche?
which?

Os vöcha Shtot kumst du?
Which city do you come from?

ia
her

Ole san kema, osa **iara** Shvesta.
Everyone came except her sister.

de
the

De Mos is in de Kuchl glofn.
The mouse ran into the kitchen.

Pronouns

PRONOUNS replace determiners and nouns:

    mai Shvesta   **si**
    my sister   she

    vöche Beason?   **vea?**
    which person?   who?

Some pronouns change after special prepositions:

    one **di**   mit **dia**
    without you   with you

    gegn **si**   osa **ia**
    against her   except her

The following are some common pronouns:

he	ea
she	si
it	es
they	se
you (singular)	du
you (plural)	es
I	i
we	mia
what?	vos?
who?	vea?
something	etvos
somebody, someone	jemond
anything	iagendvos
anybody, anyone	iagendvea
everything	ois
everybody, everyone	ole
nothing	nix
nobody, no one	nimond
this, these, that, those	des
there (there is, there were, etc)	do
there (there is, there were, etc)	es
one, you (people in general)	mo

After verbs and prepositions, we use the following pronouns:

him	**eam**
her	si
it	es
them	se
you, yourself	**di**
you, yourselves	**aich**
me, myself	**mi**
us	**uns**
herself, himself, itself, themselves, ourselves	**si**
what?	**vos?**
who?, whom?	**vem?**
something	etvos
somebody, someone	jemond
anything	iagendvos
anybody, anyone	**iagendvem**
everything	ois
everybody, everyone (plural)	ole
nothing	nix
nobody, no one	nimond

After special prepositions, we use the following pronouns:

him	**eam**
her	**ia**
it	**es**
them	**eana**
you, yourself	**dia**
you, yourselves	**aich**
me, myself	**mia**
us	**uns**
herself, himself, itself, themselves, ourselves	**si**
what?	**vos?**
who?, whom?	**vem?**
something	**etvos**
somebody, someone	**jemond**
anything	**iagendvos**
anybody, anyone	**iagendvem**
everything	**ois**
everybody, everyone (plural)	**oin**
nothing	**nix**
nobody, no one	**nimond**

Did you know?

The pronouns do and es (both meaning there) are used with the verbs san (for place) and gebn (for existence) respectively:

do is a Fro im Zima
there is a woman in the room

do san Fron im Zima
there are women in the room

es gibt fü Griminalitet in disa Shtot
there is a lot of crime in this city

es gibt füle Griminele in disa Shtot
there are a lot of criminals in this city

> Fill in the blanks!

i
I

Los __ gen!
Let me go!

du
you

Host __ no mea?
Do you have any more?

si
she

Jo, si libt __ söbst viakli.
Yeah, she really loves herself.

vea?
who?

Mit ____ is ea gonga? —Mit mia.
Who did he go with? —With me.

es
you

Es hobz ____ im Shpiagl gsegn.
You saw yourselves in the mirror.

> Here are the answers. No cheating!

i
I

    Los **mi** gen!
    Let me go!

du
you

    Host **du** no mea?
    Do you have any more?

si
she

    Jo, si libt **si** söbst viakli.
    Yeah, she really loves herself.

vea?
who?

    Mit **vem** is ea gonga? —Mit mia.
    Who did he go with? —With me.

es
you

    Es hobz **aich** im Shpiagl gsegn.
    You saw yourselves in the mirror.

Adjectives

ADJECTIVES describe nouns:

    gliklich   mai Koz is **gliklich**
    happy   my cat is happy

    gshaid   maine Briada san **gshaid**
    clever   my brothers are clever

Between a noun and a determiner, add *e* to the adjective:

    rod   de Dia is rod
    red   the door is red

                                          a rod**e** Dia
                                          a red door

    grantig   de Fro is grantig
    angry   the woman is angry

                                          de grantig**e** Fro
                                          the angry woman

With a plural noun or after special prepositions, add *en*:

raich
rich

mai Dont is raich
my aunt is rich

mai raich**e** Dont
my rich aunt

maine raich**en** Dontn
my rich aunts

osa maina raich**en** Dont
except my rich aunt

Did you know?

Some adjectives are special. When we add anything to these adjectives, they change:

she (**shen**)
beautiful

de Fro is she
the woman is beautiful

de **shen**e Fro
the beautiful woman

The following are some common adjectives:

angry	grantig
awesome	laivand
big	gros
black	shvoaz
blue	blo
clever	gshaid
cold	koid
good	guad
gray	gro
green	grian
handsome	fesh
happy	gliklich
high	hoch
hot	has
ill	gronk
long	long
near	no
new	naich
old	oid
orange	orojh
red	rod
rich	raich
sad	drorig
strong	shtoak
stupid	depat

sweet	sias
yellow	göb
young	jung

The following are some common special adjectives:

beautiful	she (**shen**)
clear	gloa (**gloar**)
fast	shnö (**shnöl**)
pink	rosa (**rosan**)
purple	lila (**lilan**)
small	gla (**glan**)

> Fill in the blanks!

sötsam strange	Da _____ Mon do hast Rumpöshtüzchen. That strange man is called Rumpelstiltskin.
sias sweet	Hensl hot in de _____ Kuchn bisn. Hansel bit into the sweet cakes.
shnö (shnöl) fast	I broch a _____ Fabindung I need a fast connection.
has hot	Is da De no ___? Is the tea still hot?
rosa (rosan) pink	I lib dai **rosane** Doshn! I'm loving your pink bag!

Here are the answers.
No cheating!

sötsam strange	Da **sötsame** Mon do hast Rumpöshtüzchen. That strange man is called Rumpelstiltskin.
sias sweet	Hensl hot in de **siasen** Kuchn bisn. Hansel bit into the sweet cakes.
shnö (shnöl) fast	I broch a **shnöle** Fabindung I need a fast connection.
has hot	Is da De no **has**? Is the tea still hot?
rosa (rosan) pink	I lib dai **rosane** Doshn! I'm loving your pink bag!

Adverbs

ADVERBS modify individual words, phrases or sentences:

es is guad
it's good

es is **ua** guad
it's very good

of disa Vöt
in this world

iagendvo of disa Vöt
anywhere in this world

i kon ned kuma
I can't come

i kon **laida** ned kuma
I can't come unfortunately

We can also use an adjective as an adverb:

longsom
slow

ea is longsom
he is slow

ea oabait **longsom**
he works slowly

The following are some common adverbs:

a few times	a boamoi
a little	a bisl
a lot (a lot warmer, etc)	fü
a lot, very much (to a great extent)	sea
absolutely	sevoi
actually	aigentlich
after all	endlich
after that	drof
after, afterwards	danoch
after, afterwards	nocha
again	nomoi
again	vida
almost, nearly	fost
already	sho
also, as well, too	a
always	ima
another time	a ondasmoi
anywhere, somewhere	iagendvo
anywhere else, somewhere else	vo ondas
anywhere, no matter where, everywhere	üvaroi
at all, really (with negation)	goa
at home, home	daham
at least	zmindest
at most	of jednfoi
at present	jezt

at the bottom	untn
at the moment	im moment
at the same time	dabai
at the same time	zglaich
at the top	obn
before, beforehand	dafua
before, beforehand	zvoa
by the way	übrigns
completely	foi
completely	voikomn
continually	oiva
currently	jezig
enough	gnua
especially	bsundrig
even (even hotter, etc)	no
even (even the man, etc)	a
extremely	sea
fairly	zimli
firstly	eastns
for a long while	long
for a short while	kuaz
for a short while	fia a vengl Zait
for hours	shtundnlong
for the time being	fuaeast
frequently	oft
from there	fo do
from there	fo duat
from where?	fo vo?
from where?, where?	vohea?
gladly	gean
here	do
herself, myself, themselves, etc	söva
herself, myself, themselves, etc	söbst
how?	vi?
how long?	vi long?
how many times?	vi oft?

how often?	vi oft?
however	ova
immediately	sofuat
immediately	glaich
in any case	jednfois
in the future	in da Zukunft
in the meantime	davail
in the middle	mitn
in the morning	in da Frua
incessantly	dauand
inside	drinen
instantly	glaich
just (in instructions)	moi
just, just now	grod jezt
later	shpeta
least (the least hot, etc)	om venigstn
less (less hot, etc)	veniga
long ago	lengst
many times	fümois
maybe, perhaps	filaicht
meanwhile	in da Zvishnzait
more and more (hotter and hotter, etc)	ima
more	mea
more gladly	liava
more often	öfta
most often	om maistn
mostly	maistns
namely	und zvoa
never	ni
never	nimois
never (on no occasion)	kamoi
nevertheless	deno
nevertheless	drozdem
no	na
not even (not even a man, etc)	nedamoi
now	grod

nowadays	haizdog
nowhere, not anywhere	niagends
nowhere, not anywhere	niagendvo
occasionally	monchmoi
often	oft
often	eftas
on the inside	inan
on the outside	osn
once (one time)	amoi
once (upon a time)	domois
once more	noamoi
only	nua
otherwise	ondanfois
outside	drosn
please	bitshe
previously	ejemois
previously	friara
probably	voi
quite	gons
rarely, seldom	sötn
really	recht
really	viakli
recently	sait kuazm
recently	fua kuazm
repeatedly	eftas
secondly	zvaitns
since when?, how long?	sait von?
sometime, sometime or other	iagendvon
sometimes	monchmoi
soon	boid
still, yet	no
thank you	donkshe
then, after that	don
then, at that time	domois
then, in that case	don
then, in that case	oiso

there	do
there	duat
thereby	daduach
therefore	des hoib
therefore	drum
therefore	des hoib
thirdly	dritns
this time	deamoi
though	ova
three times	draimoi
to where?, where?	vohi?
today	hait
tomorrow	muagn
too (too hot, etc)	zua
twice	zvamoi
umpteen times	zigmoi
until when?, how long?	bis von?
up to now	bis jezt
very soon	demnext
very	ua
very	sea
what for?, why?	fia vos?
when?	von?
where?	vo?
why?	varum?
why?	viso?
yes	jo
yesterday	gestan

Did you know?

We often use the adverbs *gean* and *liava* to denote preference:

ea get gean
he likes to go
(he goes gladly)

ea get liava
he prefers to go
(he goes more gladly)

> Fill in the blanks!

__ is mai Hendi? _____ muas es san!

I bin __ guad gvesn. Ova du bist __ besa.

I voat _____ om Flughofn.

_____ is es _____ koid.

_____ kindigst du dain Djob?

> Here are some possibilities. No cheating!

Vo is mai Hendi? **Iagendvo** muas es san!
Where is my mobile? It must be somewhere!

I bin **ua** guad gvesn. Ova du bist **no** besa.
I was very good. But you are even better.

I voat **shtundnlong** om Flughofn.
I've been waiting in the airport for hours.

Hait is es **veniga** koid.
It is less cold today.

Varum kindigst du dain Djob?
Why are you quitting your job?

Verbs

VERBS refer to actions:

donzn	dance
drinkn	drink
esn	eat
lechön	smile
shpün	play
singa	sing

In Austrian, we use verbs to talk about what we do regularly, what we're doing right now, what we will do in the future and what we have been doing up to now:

donzn	se **donzn** ima
dance	they always dance
drinkn	de Kozn **drinkn** de Müch
drink	the cats are drinking the milk
fliagn	mia **fliagn** muagn noch Vin
fly	we're flying to Vienna tomorrow
lebn	se **lebn** sho sait Joan do
live	they've been living here years

With singular subjects, change the final letter of the verb to t:

    drinkn
    drink

        de Kozn drinkn
        the cats are drinking

        de Koz drink**t**
        the cat is drinking

    shpün
    play

        se shpün
        they play

        ea shpü**t**
        he plays

With plural subjects, make the verb end in n (most verbs already do):

    lechön
    smile

        mia lechön
        we are smiling

    singa
    sing

        mia siga**n**
        we are singing

The following are some common verbs:

answer	ontvoatn
be allowed to	deafn
be supposed to	soin
believe	globn
belong to	khean
come	kuma
cook	kochn
cry	vana
dance	donzn
drink	drinkn
drive	foan
fly	fliagn
follow	foign
get, receive	griagn
go	gen
happen	basian
hear	hean
jump	shpringa
laugh	lochn
look at	shon
ought to	soin
play	shpün
please	gfoin
run	lofn
say	sogn

see	segn
show	zagn
sing	singa
sleep	shlofn
smile	lechön
study	shtudian
swim	shvima
talk	redn
tell	dazön
understand	fashten
want	voin
wash	voshn
win	gvina
work	oabaitn
would do	daradn
would like	mechatn
write	shraibn

Fill in the blanks!

liagn   Es ____ mitn im Void.
lie   It lies in the middle of the wood.

mochn   Vos _____ ea?
do   What is he doing?

oabaitn   Vo _____ si jezt?
work   Where is she working now?

vedöln   Da Hund _____ mim Shvonz.
wag   The dog is wagging his tail.

redn   Se ____ ned mit ia.
talk   They're not talking to her.

> Here are the answers. No cheating!

liagn
lie

Es liagt mitn im Void.
It lies in the middle of the wood.

mochn
do

Vos mocht ea?
What is he doing?

oabaitn
work

Vo oabait si jezt?
Where is she working now?

vedöln
wag

Da Hund vedölt mim Shvonz.
The dog is wagging his tail.

redn
talk

Se redn ned mit ia.
They're not talking to her.

Conjunctions

CONJUNCTIONS join two words, phrases or sentences together:

De **und** Kafe
tea and coffee

im Shlofzima **oda** in da Kuchl?
in the bedroom or in the kitchen?

du bist ned **so** gshaid, **vi** du denkst
you're not as clever as you think

After certain conjunctions, we usually move the verb to the end of the sentence:

si is gonga
she has gone

ea globt, **des** si gonga **is**
he believes that she has gone

The following are some common conjunctions:

and	und
as ... as	so ... vi
both ... and	sovoi ... ois
but	ova
either ... or	entveda ... oda
just as ... as	genoso ... vi
neither ... nor	und ... a ned
not as ... as	ned so ... vi
not only ... but also	ned nua ... sondan a
or	oda
than	vi

The following are some common conjunctions after which we usually move the verb to the end of the sentence:

after	nochdem
although	obvoi
as (because)	do
as if	ois ob
as long as, so long as	solong
as often as	so oft
as soon as	soboid

because	vö
before	bfua
if	von
since	sait
so that	damit
that	des
until	bis
when (in the past)	ois
when, whenever	von
whether	ob
while	verand

> Did you know?

It's becoming increasingly common NOT to move the verb to the end of the sentence after conjunctions, especially in less formal language:

> i hob ka Zait
> I don't have time

> i kum ned, **vö** i ka Zait **hob**
> I'm not coming as I don't have time

> i kum ned, vö i hob ka Zait
> I'm not coming as I don't have time

As in English, we usually drop des:

> ea hot gsogt, **des** ea noch Vin gen darad
> he said that he would go to Vienna

> ea hot gsogt, ea darad noch Vin gen
> he said he would go to Vienna

Fill in the blanks!

Domois homa si im Void faiet, ___ mia Gshropn gvesn san.

I bin in ans fo maine Fecha duachgfoin, ___ i hob main Obshluas gmocht.

Ea is __ lais __ a Mos.

___ du zaitig ofshtest, siachst du den Sunenofgong.

_____ des Veda guad is, gema ose.

> Here are some possibilities. No cheating!

Domois homa si im Void faiet, **ois** mia Gshropn gvesn san.
We got lost in the woods once, when we were children.

I bin in ans fo maine Fecha duachgfoin, **ova** i hob main Obshluas gmocht.
I failed one of my subjects, but I graduated.

Ea is **so** lais **vi** a Mos.
He is as quiet as a mouse.

Von du zaitig ofshtest, siachst du den Sunenofgong.
If you get up early, you'll see the sunrise.

Solong des Veda guad is, gema ose.
As long as the weather's good, we're going out.

Numbers

We use the following NUMBERS:

0	nui
1	ans
2	zva
3	drai
4	fia
5	fünf
6	sex
7	sibn
8	ocht
9	nai
10	zen
11	öf
12	zvöf
13	draizen
14	fiazen
15	fuchzen
16	sechzen
17	sibzen
18	ochzen
19	nainzen
20	zvanzg
30	draisg
40	fiazg
50	fufzg
60	sechzg
70	sibzg
80	ochzg

90   nainzg
100   (a)hundat
1000   (a)dosend

We create other numbers as follows:

draiazvanzg	ochtasechzg
23	68
hundatnai	fiahundatdraianainzg
109	493
fünfdosendsexhundat	sibnhundatdosend
5600	700,000

The following numbers combine with a:

ans + a	a**na**
zva + a	zva**ra**
fia + a	fia**ra**
sibn + a	si**ma**
nai + a	nai**na**
a + ochzg	**a**dochzg

sex**a**draisg	fia**ra**draisg
36	34
draiazvanzg	drai**a**dochzg
23	83

The words for million and billion are nouns:

a Milion
one million

a Miliad
one billion

drai Milion
three million

merere Miliadn
several billion

> Did you know?

In addition to counting, we can also use numbers as determiners and pronouns:

> i hob a boa Kozn
> I have a couple of cats
>
> i hob **zva** Kozn
> I have two cats
>
> i hob **zva**
> I have two

In this case, we use the determiner **a** instead of the number **ans**:

> i hob **a** Koz
> I have one cat
> (I have a cat)
>
> i hob **ans**
> I have one

The following are some numerical adjectives:

first	easte
second	zvaite
third	drite
fourth	fiate
fifth	fünfte
sixth	sexte
seventh	simte
eighth	ochte
ninth	nainte
tenth	zente
eleventh	öfte
twelfth	zvöfte
thirteenth	draizente
fourteenth	fiazente
fifteenth	fuchzente
sixteenth	sechzente
seventeenth	sibzente
eighteenth	ochzente
nineteenth	nainzente
twentieth	zvanzigste
thirtieth	draisigste
fortieth	fiazigste
fiftieth	fufzigste
sixtieth	sechzigste
seventieth	sibzigste

eightieth	ochzigste
ninetieth	nainzigste
hundredth	hundatste
thousandth	dosendste
millionth	milionste
billionth	miliadste

Say the numbers!

36 _____

768 _____

4687 _____

15070 _____

43000000 _____

Here are the answers.
No cheating!

36   sexadraisg

768   sibnhundatochtasechzg

4687   fiadosendsexhundatsimadochzg

15070   fuchzendosendsibzg

43000000   draiafiazg Milion

Part Two: More about verbs

Verbs with du, es and i

With the pronouns du, es (meaning you) and i, change the final letter of the verb as follows:

shpün
play

se shpün Fuasboi
they play football

du shpü**st** Fuasboi
you play football

es shpü**z** Fuasboi
you play football

i shpü Fuasboi
I play football

gvina
win

de Fron gvinan
the women win

du gvin**st**
you win

es gvin**z**
you win

i gvin
I win

Did you know?

The verb **san** – be is pretty irregular:

de Mena san do
the men are here

da Mon **is** do
the man is here

du **bist** do
you are here

es saz do
you are here

i **bin** do
I am here

Did you know?

The verb **hom** – have is also pretty irregular:

se hom de Orojhn
they have the oranges

si hot de Orojhn
she has the oranges

du host de Orojhn
you have the oranges

es **hobz** de Orojhn
you have the oranges

i **hob** de Orojhn
I have the oranges

Did you know?

The verb **vean** – become is also pretty irregular:

se vean grantig
they become angry

si **vead** grantig
she becomes angry

du veast grantig
you become angry

es veaz grantig
you become angry

i **vead** grantig
I become angry

Fill in the blanks!

rochn smoke	_____ du? Do you smoke?
hom have	I ___ a bisl De. I have some tea.
san be	Es ___ ua fraindlich. You're very friendly.
zvinkan wink	Varum _____ ma zua? Why are you winking at me?
soin ought to	Es ___ des naiche Gtrenk do brobian. You should try this new drink.

Here are the answers. No cheating!

rochn	Rochst du?
smoke	Do you smoke?
hom	I **hob** a bisl De.
have	I have some tea.
san	Es **saz** ua fraindlich.
be	You're very friendly.
zvinkan	Varum zvinka**st** ma zua?
wink	Why are you winking at me?
soin	Es **soiz** des naiche Gtrenk do brobian.
ought to	You should try this new drink.

Special verbs

Some verbs are SPECIAL. These verbs use a different form for singular subjects, as follows:

kina (**kon**)
be able to

mia kinan de Müch drinkn
we can drink the milk

si **kon** de Müch drinkn
she can drink the milk

du **kon**st de Müch drinkn
you can drink the milk

es kinz de Müch drinkn
you can drink the milk

i **kon** de Müch drinkn
I can drink the milk

If the singular form ends in **t**, we remove this with **i** and **du**:

gebn (**gibt**)
give

se **gebn** da des Göd
they give you the money

ea **gibt** da des Göd
he gives you the money

du **gib**st ma des Göd
you give me the money

es **gebz** ma des Göd
you give me the money

i **gib** da des Göd
I give you the money

The following are some common special verbs:

be able to	kina (**kon**)
do	dan (**duat**)
eat	esn (**ist**)
give	gebn (**gibt**)
have to	miasn (**muas**)
help	höfn (**hüft**)
know	visn (**vas**)
like to	megn (**mog**)
read	lesn (**liast**)
see	segn (**siacht**)
speak	shprechn (**shpricht**)
take	nema (**nimt**)
want	voin (**vü**)

Fill in the blanks!

esn (ist)
eat

Vos ___ si?
What is she eating?

miasn (muas)
have to

Vos _____ mia jezt dan?
What do we have to do now?

shprechn (shpricht)
be

Du _____ Östaraichish.
You speak Austrian.

gebn (gibt)
become

I ___ da des Gshenk muagn.
I'll give you the present tomorrow.

visn (vas)
know

Si ___, du bist do!
She knows you're here!

> Here are the answers. No cheating!

esn (ist)
eat

Vos **ist** si?
What is she eating?

miasn (muas)
have to

Vos **miasn** mia jezt dan?
What do we have to do now?

shprechn (shpricht)
be

Du **shprichst** Östaraichish.
You speak Austrian.

gebn (gibt)
become

I **gib** da des Gshenk muagn.
I'll give you the present tomorrow.

visn (vas)
know

Si **vas**, du bist do!
She knows you're here!

Creating nouns

We can use a verb as a noun. These nouns mean (the act of) singing, (the act of) dancing, (the act of) drinking, etc:

VERB   NOUN

singa   Singa
sing   singing

donzn   Donzn
dance   dancing

drinkn   Drinkn
drink   drinking

Obst is guad fia de Gsundhait
fruit is good for your health

Donzn is guad fia de Gsundhait
dancing is good for your health

We often use these nouns after other verbs. In this case, we don't usually capitalize them and we usually move them to the end of the sentence. The following are some of the more common ways we use these nouns:

du konst ins Vosa **shpringa**
you can jump into the water

du soist ins Vosa **shpringa**
you should jump into the water

du muast ins Vosa **shpringa**
you must jump into the water

du duast ins Vosa **shpringa**
you DO jump into the water

du host ins Vosa zum **shpringa**
you have to jump into the water

du brochst ned ins Vosa **shpringa**
you don't have to jump into the water

du veast ins Vosa **shpringa**
you will jump into the water

du veast ins Vosa **shpringa**
you are going to jump into the water

du veast ins Vosa shpringa **kina**
you will be able to jump into the water

du veast ins Vosa shpringa **miasn**
you are going to have to jump into the water

du daradst ins Vosa **shpringa**
you would jump into the water

von du ins Vosa **shpringa** daradst
if you jumped into the water

du fasuachst ins Vosa zum **shpringa**
you try to jump into the water

du siachst mi ins Vosa **shpringa**
you see me jumping into the water

du lost mi ins Vosa **shpringa**
you let me jump into the water

es is shviarig, ins Vosa zum **shpringa**
it is difficult to jump into the water

i hob a bisl Shoklad zum **esn**
I have a little chocolate to eat

i hob eam gshribn, shtot mit eam zum **shprechn**
I wrote to him instead of speaking to him

i hob gshumöt, um zum **gvina**
I cheated in order to win

i hob gshumöt, um des Spü zum **gvina**
I cheated in order to win the game

i hob gvuna, one zum **shtön**
I won without stealing

i hob gvuna, one Göd zum **shtön**
I won without stealing money

Fill in the blanks!

I muas noch Linz ____.
I have to travel to Linz.

Fo do os is da Flughofn laicht zua _____.
It's easy to get to the airport from here.

Konst du eam foan ___?
Can you let him drive?

I bin duathin gonga, um mit eam zua _____.
I went there to talk to him.

Here are the answers. No cheating!

I muas noch Linz **raisn**.
I have to travel to Linz.

Fo do os is da Flughofn laicht zua **araichn**.
It's easy to get to the airport from here.

Konst du eam foan **losn**?
Can you let him drive?

I bin duathin gonga, um mit eam zua **shprechn**.
I went there to talk to him.

Creating adjectives

We can use a verb as an adjective. To do this, add g to the verb and change the final letter to t. These adjectives mean played, done, cleaned, etc:

VERB	ADJECTIVE
shpün play	gshpüt played
mochn do	gmocht done
rainign clean	grainigt cleaned

des naiche Gvond
the new clothes

des **grainigt**e Gvond
the cleaned clothes

We often use these adjectives after the verbs **hom** and **san**. In this case, we usually move them to the end of the sentence:

i hob Fuasboi gshpüt
I played football / I have played football

i hob Fuasboi gshpüt
I had played football (you may also encounter **gshpüt ghobt**)

i vead Fuasboi gshpüt hom
I will have played football

i muas Fuasboi gshpüt hom
I must have played football

es is grainigt
it is cleaned (state: someone has already cleaned it)

es vead grainigt
it is being cleaned (action: someone is cleaning it)

Many of these adjectives are unpredictable:

gen **gonga**
go gone

shtudian **shtudiat**
study studied

With some of these adjectives, we use the verb *san* instead of *hom*:

i hob daham gshlofn
I slept at home

i **bin** daham **blibn**
I stayed at home

The following are some common unpredictable created adjectives:

answered	gontvoatet
been able to	kina
been allowed to	deafn
been obliged to	soin
been required to	miasn
cooked	kocht
done	don
drunk	drunkn
given	gebn
gotten (received)	griagt
had	ghobt
helped	ghoifn
known	gvust
liked to	megn
pleased	gfoin
read	glesn
seen	gsegn
slept	gshlofn
spoken	gshprochn
studied	shtudiat
sung	gsunga
told	dazöt
understood	fashtondn

wanted	gvoin
won	gvuna
written	gshribn

The following are some common created adjectives that are used with **san**:

been	gvesn
come	kema
driven	gfoan
flown	gflogn
gone	gonga
gotten (become)	gvoadn
happened	basiat
jumped	gshprunga
stayed	blibn
swum	gshvuma

When **gvoadn** is preceded by another created adjective, it loses its **g**:

es is has gvoadn
it has gotten hot

es is kocht **voadn**
it has been cooked

Did you know?

We can also create an adjective by changing the final letter of a verb to **at**. These adjectives mean (in the act of) singing, (in the act of) dancing, (in the act of) running, etc:

donzn
dance

donz**at**
dancing

vana
cry

van**at**
crying

Unlike in English, we don't use these adjectives after the verb **san**:

des glane Kind
the small child

des **vanat**e Kind
the crying child

des Kind vant
the child is crying

> Fill in the blanks!

kochn
cook

Ea hot ma a Supn _____.
He cooked me soup.

lesn
read

I hob füle Biachln _____.
I have read many books.

drinkn
drink

Hot ea a gnua Vosa _____?
Did he also drink enough water?

gen
go

Bist du hait sho fua de Dia _____?
Did you even go outside today?

> Here are the answers. No cheating!

kochn
cook

Ea hot ma a Supn **kocht**.
He cooked me soup.

lesn
read

I hob füle Biachln **glesn**.
I have read many books.

drinkn
drink

Hot ea a gnua Vosa **drunkn**?
Did he also drink enough water?

gen
go

Bist du hait sho fua de Dia **gonga**?
Did you even go outside today?

Inverting

As in English, we move a word or phrase to the beginning of a sentence in Austrian for emphasis or in questions. In this case, we INVERT the subject and the verb:

Erik hot endlich gvuna
Erik has finally won

endlich **hot Erik** gvuna
finally Erik has won

es gibt ned fü zua dan in disa Shtot
there's not much to do in this town

in disa Shtot **gibt es** ned fü zua dan
in this town, there's not much to do

ea is sho veg gvesn ois i eam gsegn hob
he had already gone when I saw him

ois i eam gsegn hob, **is ea** sho veg gvesn
when I saw him, he had already gone

de Fro kumt muagn
the woman is coming tomorrow

Von **kumt de Fro**?
When is the woman coming?

du vonst in Soizbuag
you live in Salzburg

Vonst du in Soizbuag?
Do you live in Salzburg?

We often drop du when inverting:

    du host eam gsegn
    you saw him

    Host **du** eam gsegn?
    Did you see him?

    Host eam gsegn?
    Did you see him?

Did you know?

When inverting, we usually combine the verb and the pronoun mia, as follows:

Mia san Hawara.
We are friends.

San mia Hawara?
Are we friends?

Sama Hawara?
Are we friends?

Mia gen ose.
We are going out.

Gen mia ose?
Are we going out?

Gema ose?
Are we going out?

Invert the following sentences!

Mia hom no Müch daham.
We have milk at home.

———————————

Des Madl faiet si.
The girl gets lost.

———————————

I mechat an naichen Djob.
I would like a new job.

———————————

> Here are some possibilities. No cheating!

Mia hom no Müch daham.
We have milk at home.

Homa no Müch daham?
Do we have milk at home?

Des Madl faiet si.
The girl gets lost.

In den Beagn **faiet si des Madl**.
The girl gets lost in the mountains.

I mechat an naichen Djob.
I would like a new job.

In da Zukunft **mechat i** an naichen Djob.
In the future, I would like a new job.

Negating

To NEGATE, use the adverb ned before the word or phrase to be negated:

blo
blue

ned blo
not blue

in maina Shtot
in my city

ned in maina Shtot
not in my city

To negate a verb, ned usually comes at the end of the sentence (before any movement):

de Koz drinkt de Müch
the cat drinks the milk

de Koz drinkt de Müch **ned**
the cat does not drink the milk

de Koz hot de Müch drunkn
the cat drank the milk

de Koz hot de Müch **ned** drunkn
the cat did not drink the milk

> Did you know?

In English, we only usually use the determiner no for emphasis. In Austrian, the equivalent determiners ka and kane are not emphatic:

>   i hob **ka** Koz gsegn
>   I didn't see a cat
>   (I saw no cat)
>
>   i hob **kane** naichen Debiche koft
>   I didn't buy any new carpets
>   (I bought no new carpets)

> Negate the following sentences!

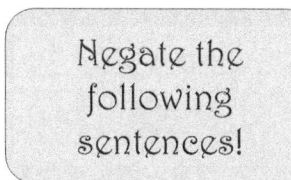

Hensl und Gretl san fo da Hex gfresn voadn.
Hansel and Gretel were eaten by the witch.

_____

Doanröshn is ofgvocht.
Sleeping Beauty woke up.

_____

De drai glanen Shvaindl hom a Laibvechtarin onghaiat.
The three little pigs have hired a bodyguard.

_____

> Here are the answers. No cheating!

Hensl und Gretl san fo da Hex gfresn voadn.
Hansel and Gretel were eaten by the witch.

Hensl und Gretl san fo da Hex **ned** gfresn voadn.

Doanröshn is ofgvocht.
Sleeping Beauty woke up.

Doanröshn is **ned** ofgvocht.

De drai glanen Shvaindl hom a Laibvechtarin onghaiat.
The three little pigs have hired a bodyguard.

De drai glanen Shvaindl hom **ka** Laibvechtarin onghaiat.

Separating

Some verbs are made up of two original words:

on	at
ruafn	call
onruafn	call (on the phone)
shpazian	walk
gen	go
shpazian gen	go for a walk

With these verbs, we SEPARATE the two words by moving the first to the end of the sentence:

onruafn	i ruaf di muagn **on**
prefer	I will call you tomorrow
shpazian gen	ea get jeden Dog **shpazian**
go for a walk	he goes for a walk every day

When we move a verb to the end of a sentence after certain conjunctions, the two words are therefore reunited:

onkuma
arrive

i kum in Vin **on**
I arrive in Vienna

von i in Vin **on**kum
when I arrive in Vienna

The following are some common verbs that we separate:

agree with	**zua**shtima
arrive	**on**kuma
assume	**on**nema (**on**nimt)
call, phone	**on**ruafn
come along	**mit**kuma
come back	**zrük**kema
cycle	**rod**foan
depart, leave	**ob**foan
get up	**of**sten
go for a walk	**shpazian** gen
go out	**os**gen
hurt	**ve**dan (**ve**duat)
join	**ba**dretn
listen	**zua**hean
pick up	**ob**hoin
shop	**an**kofn
start	**on**fonga
watch	**on**shon

123

> Did you know?

When creating nouns and adjectives, **zum** and **g** separate the two words, as follows:

i vek eam of
I wake him up

es is ima shviarig, eam of**zum**vekn
it's always difficult waking him up

i ruaf di muagn on
I will call you tomorrow

i hob di **ges**tan ongruafn
I called you yesterday

> Fill in the blanks!

onnema (onnimt)
assume

I ___ moi ___, ea is do.
I assume he's here.

ankofn
shop

_____ du hait __?
Are you shopping today?

ofshten
get up

I ____ vegn main Djob ua zaitig __.
I get up very early because of my job.

obhoin
pick up

Hait hob i si fom Banhof _____.
I picked her up from the train station today

badretn
join

I fasuach, dem Kluab _____.
I'm trying to join the club.

125

> Here are the answers. No cheating!

onnema (**on**nimt)
assume

I **nim** moi **on**, ea is do.
I assume he's here.

ankofn
shop

Kofst du hait **an**?
Are you shopping today?

ofshten
get up

I **shte** vegn main Djob ua zaitig **of**.
I get up very early because of my job.

obhoin
pick up

Hait hob i si fom Banhof **obghoit**.
I picked her up from the train station today

badretn
join

I fasuach, dem Kluab **bazuadretn**.
I'm trying to join the club.

Ghosting

After certain verbs, we use the preposition fo. However, in this case, this preposition is a GHOST – although it affects the words around it, the preposition itself does not appear:

mai Muada
my mother

fo maina Muada
from my mother

i siach mai Muada
I see my mother

i hüf (**fo**) **maina** Muada
I help my mother

de Fro
the woman

fo da Fro
from the woman

i hob a Gshenk gshikt
I sent a present

i hob (**fo**) **da** Fro a Gshenk gshikt
I sent the woman a present

In this case, mia and dia become ma and da:

fo mia	du konst **ma** ois dazön
from you	you can tell me everything
fo dia	i donk **da**
from you	I thank you

The following are some common verbs after which we use the ghost preposition fo:

agree with	**zua**shtima
answer	ontvoatn
believe (someone)	globn
belong to	ghean
fit, suit	bosn
follow	foign
forgive	fazain
give (someone)	gebn (gibt)
happen to	basian
help	höfn (hüft)
hurt	**ve**dan (**ve**duan)
listen to	**zu**hean
please	gfoin
say to	sogn
show (someone)	zagn
tell (someone)	dazön
thank	donkn

Fill in the blanks!

ia
her

I hob ____ Dochta a Biachl gebn.
I gave her daughter a book.

sai
his

Ea dazöt ____ Fraindin a Gshicht.
He tells his girlfriend a story.

de
the

Des Kind heat __ Lererin goa ned zua.
The child does not listen to the teacher at all.

di
you

Ea libt __.
He loves you.

mi
me

Ontvoat __ bitshe.
Answer me please.

> Here are the answers. No cheating!

ia
her

I hob **iara** Dochta a Biachl gebn.
I gave her daughter a book.

sai
his

Ea dazöt **saina** Fraindin a Gshicht.
He tells his girlfriend a story.

de
the

Des Kind heat **da** Lererin goa ned zua.
The child does not listen to the teacher at all.

di
you

Ea libt **di**.
He loves you.

mi
me

Ontvoat **ma** bitshe.
Answer me please.

Instructing

To give an INSTRUCTION, delete du, es and the ending st:

Du kumst in mai Zima.
You come into my room.

Kum in mai Zima!
Come into my room!

Es esz des Gmias ned.
You don't eat the vegetables.

Esz des Gmias ned.
Don't eat the vegetables.

As in English, we can retain the pronoun for emphasis. In this case, we invert:

Ea get noch Englond —Ge **DU** noch Östaraich!
He's going to England —YOU go to Austria.

I ge. Blaibz **ES** do.
I'm going. YOU stay here.

We do the same thing to give a suggestion with mia. In this case, we retain the pronoun and invert:

Mia esn a bisl Kuchn.
We eat a bit of cake.

Esn mia a bisl Kuchn!
Let's eat a bit of cake!

Esma a bisl Kuchn!
Let's eat a bit of cake!

The du instruction forms for hom and san are unpredictable:

Hob an Kafe!
Have a coffee!

Du bist a Drochn. **Sai** a Drochn.
You're a dragon. Be a dragon.

> Rewrite as instructions!

Du gibst eam zen fo zen Punktn.
You give him ten out of ten.

_____

Es lofz shnöla.
You run faster.

_____

Mia shon si an Füm on.
We see a movie.

_____

> Here are the answers.
> No cheating!

Du gibst eam zen fo zen Punktn.
You give him ten out of ten.

Gib eam zen fo zen Punktn.
Give him ten out of ten.

Es lofz shnöla.
You run faster.

Lofz shnöla!
Run faster!

Mia shon si an Füm on.
We see a movie.

Shoma si an Füm on.
Let's see a movie.

Part Three: More about nouns and adjectives

Formalizing

When a plural noun appears after a special preposition, we usually change any final *e* of a determiner to *en*:

gegn
against

gegn vöch**e** Fron?
against which women?

shtot
instead of

shtot vöch**en** Fron?
instead of which women?

We also usually add *n* to the plural noun itself — if it does not end in *n* already or in *s*:

füle Miada
many mothers

mit füle**n** Miada**n**
with many mothers

de Ötan
the parents

nebn den Ötan
next to the parents

merere Otos
several cars

zvishn merer**en** Otos
between several cars

We also usually change the following determiners:

kane	kan
maine	main
saine	sain
daine	dain
unsare	unsan
ire	ian
aichare	aichan
one	one maine Kozn
without	without my cats
noch	noch **main** Kozn
toward	toward my cats

Did you know?

These changes with plural nouns only usually occur in more FORMAL Austrian. In more everyday language, we don't usually make these changes:

> i von hinta de**n** hoche**n** Beag**n**
> I live behind the high mountains (formal)

> i von hinta de hochen Beag
> I live behind the high mountains (informal)

However, when we ghost the preposition *fo*, we do usually formalize — in order to distinguish the recipient from the object:

> maine Briada
> my brothers

> i hob (~~fo~~) **main** Briada**n** a Gshenk gshikt
> I sent my brothers a present

Formalize the following sentences!

Ea shtet zvishn saine Briada.
He is standing between his brothers.

———————————————

Da Lera shpricht oft mit de Shüla üva ire Zukunft.
The teacher often speaks with the students about their future.

————————————————————————

I hob anige naiche Biachln fia de glanen Kinda koft.
I bought some new books for the little children.

————————————————————————

> Here are the answers. No cheating!

Ea shtet zvishn saine Briada.
He is standing between his brothers.

Ea shtet zvishn **sain** Briadan.
He is standing between his brothers.

Da Lera shpricht oft mit de Shüla üva ire Zukunft.
The teacher often speaks with the students about their future.

Da Lera shpricht oft mit den Shülan üva ire Zukunft.
The teacher often speaks with the students about their future.

I hob anige naiche Biachln fia de glanen Kinda koft.
I bought some new books for the little children.

I hob den glanen Kindan anige naiche Biachln koft.
I bought the little children some new books.

Sheep and wolves

Some nouns are special in the singular. There are two groups of these special nouns. Let's call these nouns SHEEP and WOLVES (because the nouns Shof and Voif belong to the first and second group respectively):

airplane	Flugzaig
bicycle	Radl
cup	Hefl
face	Gsicht
mushroom	Shvaml
sheep	Shof

bear	Bea
cake	Kuchn
potato	Eadopfl
sky	Himl
tree	Bam
wolf	Voif

With sheep, we change any final *e* of a determiner to *es*. With wolves, we change any final *e* of a determiner to *a*:

Koz
cat

vöche Koz?
which cat?

vöche Kozn?
which cats?

Shof
sheep

vöch**es Shof**?
which sheep? (singular)

vöche Shofe?
which sheep? (plural)

Voif
wolf

vöch**a Voif**?
which wolf?

vöche Vöf?
these wolves

With both sheep and wolves, after special prepositions, we change any final *e* of a determiner to *em*:

Fro
woman

mit da Fro
with the woman

mit de Fron
with the women

Radl
bicycle

mit d**em Radl**
with the bicycle

mit de Radl
with the bicycles

Bam
tree

mit d**em Bam**
with the tree

mit de Bama
with the trees

After special prepositions, we also change the following determiners:

a	an
ka	kan
mai	main
sai	sain
dai	dain
unsa	unsan
ia	ian
aicha	aichan

nebn
next to

nebn ana Koz
next to a cat

nebn **an** Shof
next to a sheep

nebn **an** Voif
next to a wolf

The following are some common sheep:

airplane	Flugzaig
animal	Fich
bag	Sakl
bean	Bondl
bed	Bet
bedroom	Shlofzima
bicycle	Radl
biscuit	Keks
boat	Bot
book	Biachl
bread	Brot
car	Oto
chicken	Hendl
clothes	Gvond
cup	Hefl
deer	Re
ear	Oavashl
egg	Ai
eye	Og
face	Gsicht
fire	Faia
flower	Bleaml
food	Lebnsmitl
fruit	Obst
grape	Vanpl

grass	Gros
hair	Hoa
horse	Ros
house	Haisl
ice	Ais
knife	Mesa
lizard	Aidaxl
meat	Flaish
mouth	Goshl
mushroom	Shvaml
oil	Ö
photo	Büdl
plate	Döla
rabbit	Kanikl
room	Zima
salt	Soiz
sea	Mea
sheep	Shof
shelf	Kastl
ship	Shif
shirt	Hemad
spice	Gviaz
toilet	Haisl
vegetables	Gmias
vehicle	Foazaig
window	Fensta
yogurt	Joguat

Nouns referring to a child are also often sheep:

baby	Zvucgl
child	Kind
daughter	Menca
girl	Madl

150

The following are some common wolves:

apple	Opfl
arm	Oam
ball	Boi
beach	Shtrond
bear	Bea
beard	Boat
bird	Fogl
body	Köpa
bucket	Kiabl
bus	Bus
butter	Buta
cake	Kuchn
carpet	Debich
cauliflower	Kafiol
chair	Sesl
cheese	Kas
chocolate	Shoklad
coat	Montl
coffee	Kafe
computer	Kompjuta
cushion	Boista
dog	Hund
elephant	Elefont
fan	Bropela
fish	Fish

floor	Fuasbodn
foot	Fuas
forest	Void
garden	Goatn
garlic	Knofe
glove	Handshuach
hat	Huat
head	Shedl
honey	Honig
jacket	Jompa
juice	Soft
key	Shlisl
lake	Se
leg	Haxn
lion	Löve
mirror	Shpiagl
monkey	Of
moon	Mond
mountain	Beag
octopus	Dintnfish
onion	Zvife
peach	Pfeshe
potato	Eadopfl
profession	Hakn
rainbow	Regnbogn
rice	Rais
river	Flus
salad	Salot
shoe	Shuach
sky	Himl
snail	Shnek
snow	Shne
sock	Sokn
spoon	Lefl
star	Shtean
stone	Shta

storm	Shtuam
table	Dish
tea	De
tomato	Baradaisa
tooth	Zon
train	Zug
tree	Bam
wardrobe	Kostn
wind	Vind
wolf	Voif

Nouns referring to a man are also often wolves:

boy	Bua
brother	Bruada
father	Foda
friend (male)	Havara
grandfather	Grosfoda
husband	Gate
man	Mon
son	Bua
uncle	Onkl
architect (male)	Achitekt
artist (male)	Künstler
astronaut (male)	Astronot
dancer (male)	Denza
doctor (male)	Oazt
farmer (male)	Baua
hairdresser	Frisea
judge (male)	Richta
king	König
mechanic (male)	Mechanika
neighbor (male)	Nochbo

pilot (male)	Bilot
plumber (male)	Inshtalatea
police officer (male)	Kivara
secretary (male)	Sekretea
singer (male)	Senga
soldier (male)	Soidot
student (male)	Shtudent
teacher (male)	Lere
waiter (male)	Köna

Rewrite with a sheep or wolf!

De Honddoshn do is vundashe.
This handbag is lovely.

_____

Da Hos frist de Karotn.
The hare eats the carrot.

_____

De Koz is bai maina Dochta.
The cat is with my daughter.

_____

Here are some possibilities. No cheating!

De Honddoshn do is vundashe.
This handbag is lovely.

Da Goatn do is vundashe.
This garden is lovely.

Da Hos frist de Karotn.
The hare eats the carrot.

Da Hos frist **des Gros**.
The hare eats the grass.

De Koz is bai maina Dochta.
The cat is with my daughter.

De Koz is bai **main Bua**.
The cat is with my son.

Possessing

We usually use the preposition **fo** to denote POSSESSION:

des Doch **fo** dem Heisl
the roof of the house

des Oto **fo** main Bruada
the car of my brother / my brother's car

de Koz **fo** Erik
Erik's cat

We can also use a name as a determiner. To do this, add **s** to the name. These determiners mean Erik's, Mark's, Sarah's, etc:

Erik
Erik

Erik**s** Koz
Erik's cat

Julia
Julia

Julia**s** Kistn
Julia's box

We can do the same thing with nouns that denote family members:

Oma
grandmother

Omas Haisl
grandmother's house

Bapa
dad

Bapas Hund
dad's dogs

We also sometimes ghost the determiner fo to denote possession, as follows:

des Oto **fo** main Bruada
my brother's car

(~~fo~~) main Bruada sai Oto
my brother's car
(~~from~~ my brother, his car)

> Match the type of possession!

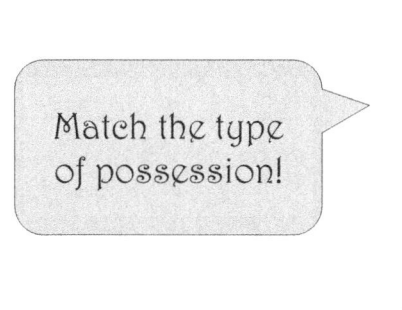

des Biro fo main Sekretea
my secretary's office

family member + s

Des is da Gebitslaitarin sai Oto.
That's the area manager's car.

fo

Vo is Susis Döla?
Where's Susi's plate?

ghosted fo

Mamas Honddoshn föt.
Mom's purse is missing.

name + s

Here are the answers. No cheating!

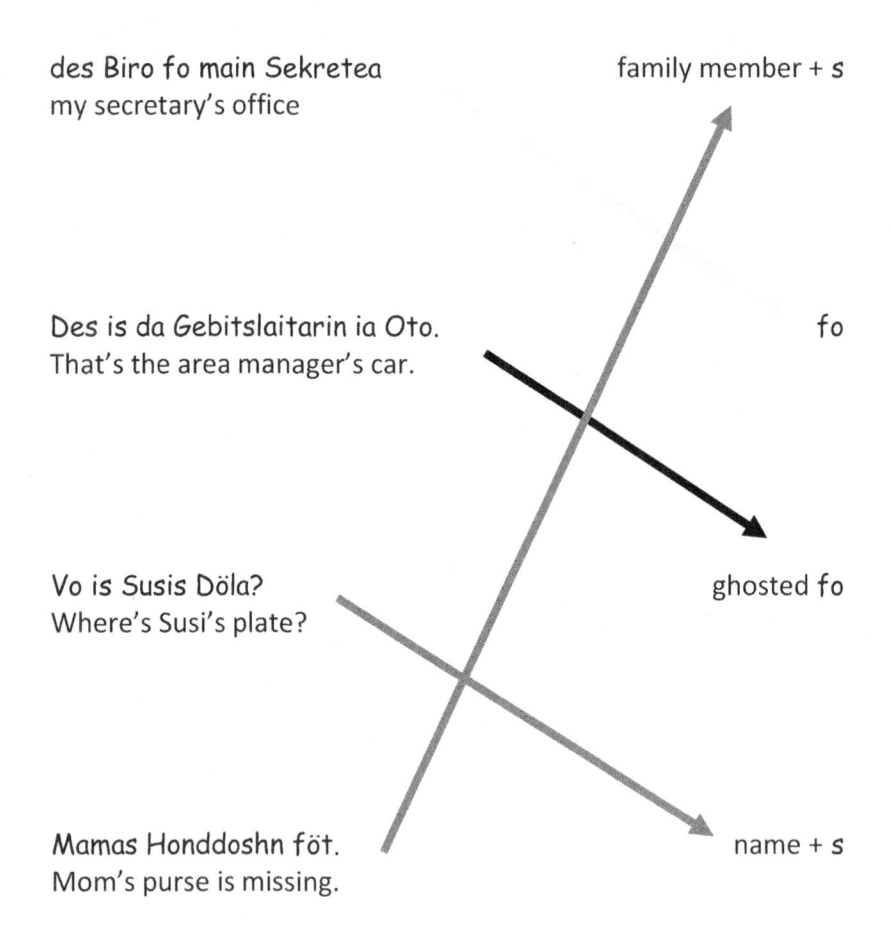

des Biro fo main Sekretea
my secretary's office

family member + s

Des is da Gebitslaitarin ia Oto.
That's the area manager's car.

fo

Vo is Susis Döla?
Where's Susi's plate?

ghosted fo

Mamas Honddoshn föt.
Mom's purse is missing.

name + s

Comparing

To COMPARE, add **a** or **st** to adjectives:

grantig
angry

grantig**a**
angrier

grantig**st**
angriest

We use comparative forms like normal adjectives. However, comparative forms with **a** are special adjectives:

fesh
handsome

da fesh**e** Bua
the handsome boy

feshst
most handsome

i bin da fehsh**te** Bua in da Klosn
I am the handsomest boy in the class

fesha (**feshar**)
more handsome

i bin fesha vi mai Bruada
I am more handsome than my brother

i bin da **feshar**e Bruada
I am the more handsome brother

Some comparative forms are unpredictable:

shtoak	**shteaka**
strong	stronger

guad	**best**
good	best

The following are some common adjectives with unpredictable comparative forms:

gronk	grenka	grenkst
gros	gresa	grest
guad	**besa**	**best**
hoch	hecha	hechst
jung	jünga	jüngst
koid	köda	ködest
long	lenga	lengst
no	**nea**	neast
oid	öda	ödest
shtoak	shteaka	shteakst

Did you know?

Like other adjectives, we can also use a comparative form as an adverb (note the form with om ...n):

shnö (shnöl)
quick

ea loft shnö
he runs quickly

ea loft shnöla
he runs more quickly

ea loft **om** shnölst**n**
he runs the quickest

Fill in the blanks!

bülig cheap	De Zaitshrift is _____ vi i docht hob. The magazine is cheaper than I thought.
jung young	Mai _____ Dochta get jezt zua Shui. My younger daughter is going to school now.
longsom slow	Ea loft _____. He runs the slowest.
oid old	Des Madl is mit dem _____ Kind do. The girl is here with the oldest child.
lot loud	Ea singt ___. He sings more loudly.

Here are the answers.
No cheating!

bülig cheap	De Zaitshrift is büliga vi i docht hob. The magazine is cheaper than I thought.
jung young	Mai **jüngare** Dochta get jezt zua Shui. My younger daughter is going to school now.
longsom slow	Ea loft **om** longsom**stn**. He runs the slowest.
oid old	Des Madl is mit dem **ödesten** Kind do. The girl is here with the oldest child.
lot loud	Ea singt lota. He sings more loudly.

Donating

When an adjective appears before a noun but there is no determiner, then imagine that the adjective is preceded by the determiner de. This determiner then DONATES its endings to the adjective:

de voame Müch
the warm milk

voame Müch
warm milk

de voamen Hend
the warm hands

voame Hend
warm hands

mit da voamen Müch
with the warm milk

mit voama Müch
with warm milk

des gloare Vosa
the clear water

gloares Vosa
clear water

in dem koiden Vosa
in the cold water

in koidem Vosa
in cold water

We also usually donate after determiners that do NOT end in *e*:

da siase Kuchn
the sweet cake

siasa Kuchn
sweet cake

mai siasa Kuchn
my sweet cake

mit **dem** frishen Bluad
with the fresh blood

mit frishem Bluad
with fresh blood

mit **a bisl** frishem Bluad
with a bit of fresh blood

> Fill in the blanks!

shviarig
difficult

Des san viakli _____ Frogn.
These are really difficult questions.

hö (höl)
bright

Es is a _____ Muagn gvesn.
It was a brighter morning.

dif
deep

Si hot eam mit _____ Hos ongshot.
She looked at him with deep hatred.

naich
new

Mia hom ned gnua _____ Oatikl.
We don't have enough new items.

long
long

noch drai _____ Shtundn
after three long hours

> Here are the answers. No cheating!

shviarig
difficult

Des san viakli shviarige Frogn.
These are really difficult questions.

hö (höl)
bright

Es is a hölara Muagn gvesn.
It was a brighter morning.

dif
deep

Si hot eam mit dif**em** Hos ongshot.
She looked at him with deep hatred.

naich
new

Mia hom ned gnua naiche Oatikl.
We don't have enough new items.

long
long

noch drai long**en** Shtundn
after three long hours

Ghosting nouns

We can use adjectives as nouns. These nouns mean that red one, the long one, an interesting one, etc. To do this, ghost the noun and capitalize the adjective:

    de rode Dia   de **Rode**
    the red door   the red one

    mit unsan longen Dish   mit unsan **Longen**
    with our long table   with our long one

    a interesonteres Biachl   a **Interesonteres**
    a more interesting book   a more interesting one

In the same way, we can use determiners as pronouns. These pronouns mean mine, theirs, this one, etc. Again, ghost the noun:

    i hob daine Keks gesn
    I ate your cookies

    i hob **daine** gesn
    I ate yours

Vöcha Bua hot gvuna?
Which boy won?

Vöcha hot gvuna?
Which one has won?

When ghosting nouns, the determiner da becomes dea and the formal determiner den becomes denen:

de Kistn do san naich
these boxes are new

de (~~Kistn~~) do san naich
these are new

Vo is da Kivara? —Da Kivara is do.
Where is the policeman? —The policeman is here.

Vo is da Kivara? —**Dea** (~~Kivara~~) is do.
Where is the policeman? —He is here.

se san hinta den Otos do
they're behind those cars

se san hinta **denen** (~~Otos~~) do
they're behind those ones

> **Rewrite with a ghost!**

Vea gvint? —De naichen Shpüla.
Who's winning? —The new players.

_____

Vo is da bloe Jompa, den i koft hob?
Where's the blue jacket I bought?

_____

I hob a naiches Hendi. Vöches Hendi favendst?
I have a new mobile. Which mobile are you using?

_____

> Here are the answers. No cheating!

Vea gvint? —De naichen Shpüla.
Who's winning? —The new players.

Vea gvint? —De **Naichen**.
Who's winning? —The new ones.

Vo is da bloe Jompa, den i koft hob?
Where's the blue jacket I bought?

Vo is da **Bloe**, den i koft hob?
Where's the blue one I bought?

I hob a naiches Hendi. Vöches Hendi favendst?
I have a new mobile. Which mobile are you using?

I hob a naiches Hendi. **Vöches** favendst?
I have a new mobile. Which are you using?

Parachuting

When a wolf appears after a verb or (non-special) preposition, we first imagine that wolf is a formal plural noun. We then PARACHUTE in any determiners and adjectives, as follows:

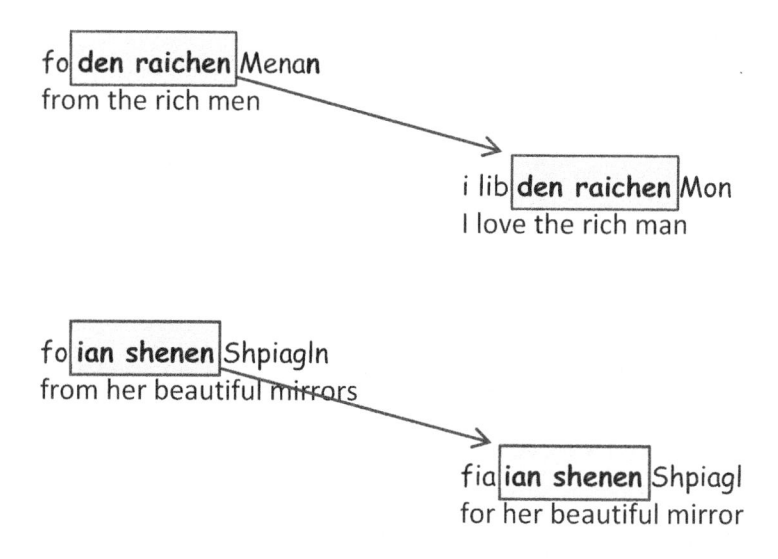

fo **den raichen** Menan
from the rich men

→ i lib **den raichen** Mon
I love the rich man

fo **ian shenen** Shpiagln
from her beautiful mirrors

→ fia **ian shenen** Shpiagl
for her beautiful mirror

Instead of the determiner a, we use an:

a naicha Debich
a new carpet

i hob **an** naichen Debich
I have a new carpet

We don't parachute after the verb *san*:

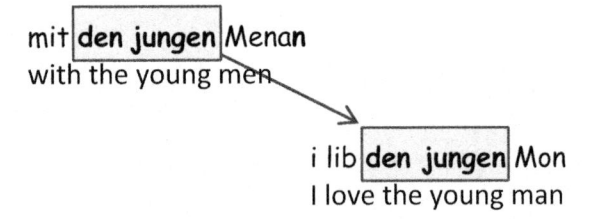

mit **den jungen** Menan
with the young men

i lib **den jungen** Mon
I love the young man

i bin da junge Mon
I am the young man

Host no _____ Kuchn gesn?
Have you eaten your white cake yet?

fia _____ Mon in Bresbuag
for the most handsome man in Bratislava

I hob __ Bea im Void gsegn.
I saw a bear in the woods.

Si hot of _____ Kivara gshosn.
She shot at the young policeman.

Ea is ___ Havara gvesn.
He was my friend.

> Here are the answers. No cheating!

Host no **dain vaisen** Kuchn gesn?
Have you eaten your white cake yet?

fia **den feshsten** Mon in Bresbuag
for the most handsome man in Bratislava

I hob **an** Bea im Void gsegn.
I saw a bear in the woods.

Si hot of **den jungen** Kivara gshosn.
She shot at the young policeman.

Ea is mai Havara gvesn.
He was my friend.

Combining

When certain words appear together, we can COMBINE the two. We have already seen this with numbers and verbs with mia:

zva + a   **zvara**zvanzg
                       twenty two

san + mia   **Sama** Havara?
                       Are we friends?

The following are some other common combinations:

in + de	ind
zua + da	zua
bai + den	bain
duach + den	duachn
hinta + den	hintan
unta + den	untan
üva + den	üvan
duach + des	duachs
fia + des	fias
fua + des	fuas
hinta + des	hintas
in + des	ins
of + des	ofs
on + des	ons
um + des	ums
unta + des	untas
üva + des	üvas

bai + dem	baim
fo + dem	fom
fua + dem	fuam
hinta + dem	hintam
in + dem	im
mit + dem	mim
noch + dem	nochm
on + dem	om
osa + dem	osam
sait + dem	saitm
unta + dem	untam
üva + dem	üvam
zua + dem	zum

With the pronoun *es* (meaning it):

fia + es	dafia
fo + es	dafo
fua + es	dafua
gegn + es	dagegn
hinta + es	dahinta
in + es	drin
mit + es	damit
nebn + es	danebn
of + es	drof
on + es	dron
os + es	dros
unta + es	drunta
üva + es	drüva
zua + es	dazua
zvishn + es	dazvishn

Did you know?

We can also combine the pronoun *es* (meaning it) with a previous verb, as follows:

i hob es sho don
I have already done it

i hob's sho don
I have already done it

Vi get es da?
How are you?

Vi get's da?
How are you?

> Fill in the blanks!

I _____ sait da Faia ned gsegn.
I haven't seen it since the party.

Vos _____ heit Nocht?
What are we doing tonight?

Is Obst ____ Moakt besa?
Is fruit from the market better?

Ea is __ Bodezima.
He's in the bathroom.

_____ Shlos Shenbrun.
Let's go to Schönbrunn Palace.

> Here are the answers. No cheating!

I **hob's** sait da Faia ned gsegn.
I haven't seen it since the party.

Vos **mochma** heit Nocht?
What are we doing tonight?

Is Obst **fom** Moakt besa?
Is fruit from the market better?

Ea is **im** Bodezima.
He's in the bathroom.

Gema zum Shlos Shenbrun.
Let's go to Schönbrunn Palace.

Misgendering

The pronouns *ea*, *si* and *es* denote he, she and it respectively:

De Fro? **Si** is im Vonzima.
The woman? She is in the living room.

Da Mon is im Void gshtondn. **Ea** is ua oid gvesn.
The man stood in the forest. He was very old.

Des Shif is kopuat gvesn, ois **es** zrükkema is.
The ship was broken when it came back.

However, if a singular noun can appear with *da*, *de* or *des*, we usually MISGENDER it by using *ea*, *si* and *es* respectively:

De Vos? **Si** is im Vonzima.
The vase? It is in the living room.
(The vase? She is in the living room.)

Da Bam is im Void gshtondn. **Ea** is ua oid gvesn.
The tree stood in the forest. It was very old.
(The tree stood in the forest. He was very old.)

Des Madl is gronk gvesn, ois **es** zrükkema is.
The girl was ill when she came back.
(The girl was ill when it came back.)

Did you know?

We have a similar thing in English. In English, we often misgender ships and countries as women:

> We just got a new boat, and I can't wait to take **her** out on the water.

> Canada is known for **her** picturesque landscapes. In winter, **she** is a snow-covered wonderland.

We also refer to a person in the plural when we don't know or don't care what gender they are:

> Someone left **their** jacket at the party. I hope **they** come back to get it.

> When a student is late for class, **they** should explain why.

> Fill in the blanks!

Da naiche Kafe is guad. __ hot fü Gshmok.
The new coffee is nice. It has a lot of flavor.

Vöche Foab hot de Vond do? —__ is gro.
What color is that wall? —It's gray.

I lib den Boak do - __ is so no on main Haisl.
I love this park – it's so close to my house.

Des Zvucgl vant vida - i glob __ hot Hunga.
The baby is crying again – I think he's hungry.

I broch a naiche Lompn. I shtö __ in main Zima.
I need a new lamp. I'm going to put it in my room.

Here are the answers. No cheating!

Da naiche Kafe is guad. **Ea** hot fü Gshmok.
The new coffee is nice. It has a lot of flavor.

Vöche Foab hot de Vond do? —**Si** is gro.
What color is that wall? —It's gray.

I lib den Boak do - **ea** is so no on main Haisl.
I love this park – it's so close to my house.

Des Zvucgl vant vida - i glob **es** hot Hunga.
The baby is crying again – I think he's hungry.

I broch a naiche Lompn. I shtö **si** in main Zima.
I need a new lamp. I'm going to put it in my room.

Identifying

We can IDENTIFY which noun we are talking about by giving extra information about that noun. To do this, we create the pronoun de by ghosting the noun, as follows:

    de Fro singt a Liad   **de (~~Fro~~) singt a Liad**
    the woman sings a song

    de Fro, de a Liad singt
    the woman who sings a song

    i lib den Mon om maistn   i lib **den (~~Mon~~) om maistn**
    I love the man the most

    da Mon, den i om maistn lib
    the man (that) I love the most

    mia singan mit den Gshropn   mia singan mit **denen (~~Gshropn~~)**
    we sing with the children

    de Gshropn, mit denen mia singan
    the children (whom) we sing with

As in English, **des** often becomes **vos**:

> des Biachl, des i glesn hob
> the book (that) I have read

> des Biachl, **vos** i glesn hob
> the book (what) I have read

To say whose, we use **deren**. With sheep and wolves, we use **desen**:

> de Kinda, **deren** Foda ned do gvesn is
> the children whose father was not there

> des Madl, **desen** Muada gronk is
> the girl whose mother is ill

> da Mon, **desen** Foda ned do gvesn is
> the man whose father was not there

Did you know?

As in English, with certain nouns, we can use instead adverbs:

des Shlos, **vo** mia gvont hom
the castle where we lived

da Dog, **vo** mia den Zug eavisht hom
the day we caught the train

de Oat, **vi** ea hait singt
the way he sings today

da Grund, **varum** ea singt
the reason why he sings

Did you know?

In English, we only usually use commas when we are giving extra information about a noun but not specifically identifying it. In Austrian, we usually use commas in both cases:

> Mai Shvesta, de in da Shvaiz lebt, is raich.
> My sister who lives in Switzerland is rich.
> (I have more than one sister.)

> Mai Shvesta, de in da Shvaiz lebt, is raich.
> My sister, who lives in Switzerland, is rich.
> (You don't know how many sisters I have.)

> Finish the sentences!

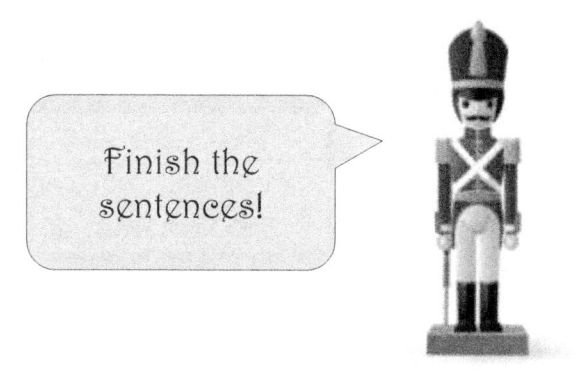

I erina mi on den Dog, _____.
I remember the day _____.

Des Oto, _____, is 12 Joa oid.
The car _____ is 12 years old.

Des is de Fro, _____.
That is the woman _____.

Des is des Gsheft, _____.
That is the store _____.

De Fro, _____, is raich.
The woman _____ is rich.

> Here are some possibilities. No cheating!

I erina mi on den Dog, **on dem i di kenagleant hob**.
I remember the day I met you.

Des Oto, **des i koft hob**, is 12 Joa oid.
The car I bought is 12 years old.

Des is de Fro, **de gestan im Restoront gvesn is**.
That is the woman who was in the restaurant yesterday.

Des is des Gsheft, **vo i main Jompa koft hob**.
That is the store where I bought my jacket.

De Fro, **dea des Oto gheat**, is raich.
The woman who owns the car is rich.

Vanishing

When we add anything to a word, if the addition is the same as the ending of the word, the addition VANISHES. We've already seen this with nouns:

Koz
cat

Kozn
cats

Karotn
carrot

Karotn
carrots (NOT karotnn)

This also happens with verbs:

oabaitn
work

si oabait
she works (NOT oabaitt)

esn (ist)
eat

du ist
you eat (NOT isst)

donzn
dance

es donz
you dance (NOT donzz)

The addition t also vanishes after d:

findn	si find
find	she finds (NOT find**t**)
redn	ea red
talk	he talks (NOT red**t**)

> Fill in the blanks!

voatn
wait

Ea ____ of den Bus.
He waits for the bus.

sitzn
sit

Vo ____ es?
Where are you sitting?

shikn
send

Si ____ iara Shvesta des Göd.
She sends her sister the money.

hasn
be called

Vi ____ du?
What are you called?

oabaitn
work

Ea hot gestan daham ____.
He worked at home yesterday.

> Here are the answers. No cheating!

voatn
wait

Ea **voat** of den Bus.
He waits for the bus.

sitzn
sit

Vo **sitz** es?
Where are you sitting?

shikn
send

Si **shikt** iara Shvesta des Göd.
She sends her sister the money.

hasn
be called

Vi **hast** du?
What are you called?

oabaitn
work

Ea hot gestan daham **goabait**.
He worked at home yesterday.

Respecting

If we are speaking to one or more people we want to show RESPECT to, we usually refer to them as they (note the capital letter):

Vohi gen se?
Where are they going?

Vohi gen **Se**?
Where are you going?

I bin mit eana gonga.
I went with them.

I bin mit **Eana** gonga.
I went with you.

Des is ia Oto.
That's their car.

Des is **Ia** Oto.
That's your car.

When instructing, we retain the pronoun and invert. We also often combine Se, as follows:

Se gen noch Graz.
You are going to Graz.

Gen Se noch Graz.
Go to Graz.

Gen'S noch Graz.
Go to Graz.

Did you know?

We used to have a singular and plural you in English:

> **du** host an Fish gesn
> **thou** host eaten a fish (singular)
>
> **es** hobz an Fish gesn
> **you** have eaten a fish (plural)

Over time, we began to use the plural you to show respect to one person, until we just used the plural with everyone. However, when showing respect in Austrian, we don't even use you:

> **Se** hom an Fish gesn
> you have eaten a fish
> (**they** have eaten a fish)

> Rewrite with respect!

Host mi fuahea ongruafn?
Did you call me earlier?

_____

Vohea kuman daine Ötan?
Where do your parents come from?

_____

Intresiaz es aich fia mai Ongebot?
Are you interested in my proposal?

_____

> Here are the
> answers.
> No cheating!

Host mi fuahea ongruafn?
Did you call me earlier?

Hom'S mi fuahea ongruafn?

Vohea kuman daine Ötan?
Where do your parents come from?

Vohea kuman **Ire** Ötan?

Intresiaz es aich fia mai Ongebot?
Are you interested in my proposal?

Intresian **Se si** fia mai Ongebot?

Remember to listen to the audio files!

https://tinyurl.com/2s4ep29z

Please also contact me with any questions, comments or suggestions!

david.young@email.com

Printed in Great Britain
by Amazon